ISBN - 978-1-300-15876-9
® R692-16438 – **Protect rite**

Cover Design: Lulu
Project Editor: Daniel Nored
Assistant Editor: Lisa McLean
Publisher: A2H Productions
Consultant Editors:
Min. Zenoviaf Maddox & Dr. Connie Holloway

The

Hook Up

By Cathy Nored

TABLE OF CONTENTS

Dedication 5

Introduction 6

Excuses, Excuses 13

No Prayer Language 13

Why Can't We Pray To God in English? 17

Strongholds and Condemnation 24

Unclean, Unworthy or Unbelieving 24

How Have We Been Programmed 28

Deliverance 32

Clean Vessels through Deliverance 32

Fear or Faith 40

Prayer Warriors 43

Don't Give the Holy Spirit 43

TABLE OF CONTENTS (Continued)

Can Help Lead Us There 47

Just Do It! 51

Hook Up Assessment 57

Important Spiritual Dates 62

Additional Ways to Maintain 63

Counting Blessings 64

Bibliography 65

Other Books Available 66

Dedication

I would like to dedicate this booklet first and foremost to my Heavenly Father and to give Him all the praise and glory for the souls that are positively impacted as a result of it. I have planted and watered, but only you, Oh God, can grant the increase! I give you my heartfelt gratitude for giving me the talent and the anointing to put words of power on these pages.

I also want to dedicate this book to my mother, Annie Marie (Long) Johnson, who—in her wisdom—instilled the importance of prayer within me. She led by example, praying no less than 3 times a day for as long as I can remember. She is also the one who passed her love of writing onto my siblings and me. Although she is no longer here in the earthly realm, her presence and her life lessons will never be forgotten. Thank you Mom, I love you.

Introduction

Today, there are many suppliers out there that offer the capability of receiving additional television channels through satellite dishes, fiber optics or cable. Most of those supplier services are so expensive that in inner-city neighborhoods there are those who cannot afford to pay their fees. People who are short on cash either have to do without the service or find a ***hook up***. A ***hook up*** is an urban term used to define people helping others to get desired services or products for free. While, I am not condoning this concept, I am using it to illustrate my point. With a ***hook up,*** those who wish to be connected to the cable supplier or provider can receive benefits without being charged after paying that one time ***hook up*** fee. Oh yes, and one more thing; anyone that was attempting to get the ***hook up*** would have to have a television ready to receive the signal.

While I was meditating on this worldly principle, the inspiration and the name for booklet came forth: The Holy Ghost Hookup. As it is often said, "as it is in the natural, so it is in the Spirit."

God provided us with Jesus who paid the price for our sins (past, present and future) once and for all. This was done so we could enjoy salvation and have ***free access*** to the additional benefits of the Kingdom through the Holy Ghost. Also, in the Body of Christ there are people (known as prayer warriors) that God has blessed with the ***gift*** of faith (not to be confused with the measure of faith). These spirit-filled warriors are ready and willing to join their faith gift with ours and give us easier access to the "Holy Ghost ***Hook Up***". The Baptism of the Holy Spirit is actually the ***Holy Ghost Hook Up*** of which I am referring to. But please note that any believer can pray with a candidate or the candidate can even pray alone. However, these prayer warriors consistently walk in the gift of faith. As a result of that God-given calling or gift, when they lay hands on people to receive the baptism the results are almost always successful.

The Bible tells us that the baptism of the Holy Spirit is available to ALL believers. However, like the example of the television, we ALL have to be ready and willing to RECEIVE the baptism through Him. And I say ***Him*** and not ***it*** because we should always remember that the Holy Spirit is the third person manifested in the Godhead. He is the one that intercedes, guides and helps us to tap into the ultimate provider: God Almighty.

Please notice that although the concepts I am presenting in this booklet may sound fairly simple, they can be convoluted by other inner-issues. Often we feel that we just can't access God in this manner; we feel we are not worthy, we might feel as if it doesn't take all that, we could feel our sins are cutting us off from the blessings, and so many of us just feel *fear*. We desire the baptism but for whatever reasons have not been able to make that powerful connection.

In this booklet, I will discuss in detail many reasons people (candidates) have not ***hooked up*** and why we may be experiencing some hindrances ***hooking up*** to the power source. I will share how we, as believers, can access the baptism of the Holy Spirit on our own or by laying hands on other believers for them to receive. I also will discuss the prayer warriors who operate in the gift of faith (I Corinthians 12:9- ***To another faith by the same Spirit****...*) and are called specifically to help those who desire the Holy Ghost ***Hook Up.*** I will talk about what these gifted faith warriors ***can*** and **cannot** be expected to do.

Having worked with people and joining my gift of faith with theirs to receive the Baptism of the Holy Spirit since 1991, I felt that it is time for me to share some of the things I have observed and learned over the years.

Last year, I wrote another reference booklet about what to do AFTER receiving the baptism of the Holy Spirit. Now I feel as though I may have "put the cart before the horse" so to speak. I am now backtracking, with this booklet, to make sure we are all aware of the things that can hinder the ***hook up*** to the Holy Ghost because many people get discouraged and **never** receive. As a spiritual prayer warrior, I have found it is best to know the "MO" and tactics of the enemy when fighting to win. To effectively accomplish my goal, myths and erroneous mindsets must also be exposed. What I share through this booklet will ensure that anyone who wants the Holy Ghost h***ook up*** WILL obtain it.

Excuses, Excuses

Already Have the Baptism of the Holy Spirit but No Prayer Language

The person who says this is not only in error but is actually trying to make excuses for not receiving something that holds the added benefit of a greater anointed prayer life. I can't begin to tell you how many people have said this to me over the years. The list ranges from pastors to politicians and from the poverty-stricken to the prosperous. Yet the Bible states in Acts 19: 6, *"**And when Paul had laid his hands upon them, The Holy Ghost came on them: and they spoke with tongues*** **[emphasis added**: Heavenly prayer language], ***and they prophesied.***" This is a point I always stress to the candidates. When we receive the baptism of the Holy Ghost, we ALWAYS receive the prayer language simultaneously as an initial sign. This makes perfect sense to me because if I had a friend who only spoke one language and suddenly started speaking in another language without studying to speak it or receiving instruction, that would definitely be an initial sign that something supernatural had occurred. So, another caveat to this is that the tongues are proof to the unbelievers. (I Corinthians 14:22) ***So then, tongues are a sign not for the believers but for unbelievers.*** It signifies to others that the Baptism of Holy Ghost has indeed happened much lie a wedding ring signifies that people are married.

There are other Biblical accounts of this correlating action, however, I want to first share a ***nugget*** that a preacher once shared with me to drive my point home. He said, "People get too caught up on getting the tongues when talking about the baptism of the Holy Ghost. When you buy a new pair of sneakers, you don't open up the box to check the shoes because you already know the tongues come with them!" We can also be assured through several examples in God's Word that the heavenly prayer language is the initial sign of the baptism of the Holy Spirit. We can read about some of those examples in the following passages:

Acts 8:17-19; Acts 10:46; Acts 11:15; Mark 16:17

If God's Word said it, then that should settle it. I, for one, believe His Word.

Why Can't We Just Pray To God in English?

Sure we could do that. We ALL can and most likely ***do*** pray in English but sometimes our natural prayers are limited by weaknesses, hindrances, emotions/sins, selfishness and unknown barriers.

Weak Prayers - At all times our prayers through the Holy Spirit are **empowered** prayers. There is no such thing as weak, faithless prayers when praying in the Spirit. In fact, the Bible tells us that we "***shall receive power***" after receiving the baptism of the Holy Ghost (Acts 1:8).

At a tent meeting years ago, a woman came up for prayer to receive the baptism of the Holy Spirit. Her husband came up when I started to lay hands on her and pray, demanding that I stop immediately. He told me she suffered from epileptic seizures. I assured him that she would be fine and that she was "in God's hands." So he reluctantly allowed me to continue without further interruption. Wouldn't you know it, this woman started having a seizure and fell on the ground in front of me? I remember praying, "God you would not have your word return back void. Please don't allow this woman to swallow her tongue." We were outside and there was nothing in that tent to even hold down her tongue. Then, I started praying for her in my prayer language and she stopped having the seizure. Next, she began to speak forth in an exceedingly clear prayer language. The Holy Spirit took control of her tongue! I am convinced that this situation could have ended very differently if I had not stood on God's Word and prayed in my Heavenly language with God's power.

Hindrances - At other times, our prayers can be hindered or delayed by the enemy [Satan]. Through God's Word we are told that the enemy held up Daniel's prayers for 21 days (Daniel 10:13). So another benefit of having a prayer language is that Satan cannot understand what we are praying for and therefore can't hinder our prayers. Our prayers will go up in a direct path to our Father God. (I Corinthians 14:2 – ***For he that speaks in an unknown tongue speaks not unto men, but unto God…)***

Emotions/Sins -Now there is a time when the enemy can actually be ***US***. This can happen when we are not in the right frame of mind to pray because of emotions like anger, hurt, or disappointment. It can also happen if we are in sin. These internal components can seriously impede prayers that are prayed in English. (I Peter 3:7) ***Likewise, you husbands dwell with them according to knowledge, giving honor unto the wife, as unto the weaker vessel, and as being heirs together of the grace of life; that your prayers be not hindered.*** Listen, wives and singles, we know that this scripture is not just for the husbands, right? If we allow emotions like strife in, it hinders our prayers.

Selfish Prayers - Finally, without a prayer language, we can only pray "natural"—often-selfish—prayers. Our prayers cannot extend past our own intellect or knowledge. Having the baptism gives us the ***hook up*** to pray supernaturally, praying prayers that are selfless and precise. Why…because the Holy Spirit is giving us what to pray while helping us to pray in perfect unison with the mind and will of God. (Romans 8:26) ***Likewise the Spirit also helps our infirmities: for we know not what we should pray for as we ought: but the Spirit itself makes intercession for us with groanings which cannot be uttered.***

Unknown Barriers - I remember praying once in the *natural* (in my own intellect and knowledge) for a young lady who wanted to receive the baptism of the Holy Spirit so badly. She did not receive until I started praying in the Spirit for her and then the Holy Spirit revealed to me that she needed to let out a war cry. When I shared this with her, she cried out loudly and received the baptism almost immediately. Up until that point her prayers were barely audible. Later she shared that she could totally relate to the term "war cry" and from that point she stopped *trying* to receive and just received the baptism of the Holy Spirit. Just the benefit of the Holy Spirit instructing and giving us knowledge should inspire us to want to accept the Holy Ghost Hook up. In my "Now

What" booklet, I address what happens AFTER receiving the baptism. In it, I also go into greater detail about the benefits of having the baptism of the Holy Spirit.

For now, suffice it to say that we should earnestly seek to pray in our Heavenly language and allow this heavenly ***hook up*** to take us higher.

Strongholds And Condemnation

Unclean, Unworthy or Unbelieving

These three **hookup**-hindering hurdles can be easily overcome. We can overcome them through the power of Faith, the Blood of Jesus, and the Holy Ghost. Generally, when I work with people to receive the Baptism of the Holy Spirit, I often tell them, "At the moment you believe, you will receive." For many ***hooking up*** is simply a matter of belief. That is why it is so important to learn what God's Word says about our areas of struggle and to continually listen and hear His Word in ours ears until our faith level has increased to be able to fully receive. The Bible says that faith comes by hearing God's Word. So what does His

Holy Word say about our receiving the Baptism of the Holy Spirit? It tells us that if we turn from our sins, (REPENT) He promises that we ***"shall receive the gift of the Holy Ghost. For the promise is unto you and to your children..."*** Acts 2:38b-39a. That means for us that the promise is a done deal. Knowing this often prompts us to ask self-evaluating questions within ourselves like ***are we worthy? Are we ready? Are we clean enough?*** In other words, we reason that if the problem is not on God's end then it MUST be on ours. These doubt-ridden questions will often vex our spirits or make us feel inadequate and uncertain when trying to make that decision to go for the ***Hook Up.*** Yet, we can always overcome these vexations and satanic strongholds though confessing, purging, renouncing and deliverance. If we find ourselves at this point, the exclusion of two major things could hinder us from moving successfully forward: **Repenting** and **Forgiving**.

Recently, I prayed with a young lady who was riddled with guilt for having fallen in her walk with God on more than one occasion. I prayed in the spirit and it was revealed she was having difficulties forgiving herself. When I shared this with her, she readily admitted it. I told her that she was being harder on herself than God was on her. After repenting and forgiving herself, I told her she was not only forgiven but I further shared that God was going to bless her through her receiving the baptism of the Holy Spirit to have the power to walk victoriously from that point on. There are times when forgiving ourselves is even harder than forgiving others. Yet, the Bible tells us that as believers all of our sins are covered under the Blood of Jesus (Read 1 John 1:9). Repent and keep going forward to obtain God's best. We must be willing and ready to leave **everything** at the altar of prayer. By sharing this story with you it is also my intention to illustrate a time when having trained prayer warriors present to help us past pivotal barriers can also be beneficial.

How Have We Been Programmed?

For a moment let's go back to my original example so that I can bring out another point. I have been told that some cable companies set up codes within their converter boxes that inhibit the reception of certain premium channels to prevent those channels from being received. They also can use scrambler signals to prevent access to the ***paid*** programming. Satan operates in much the same way to keep us from receiving God's best for us. There are benefits we are partakers of that Jesus has paid for on our behalf. However the devil has put codes (programmed messages) into our minds and assigned spirits that block us from accepting the ***hook up*** from The Holy Spirit. He sends us coded messages like, "You are not good enough, you are not clean, you lie too much, you are a sinner, you masturbate, you are an alcoholic, you are a loser and a failure, you're strung out on drugs, now ***you*** know you can't do without sex, you know you are "shacking up" with someone, you are a homosexual, you have a profane mouth, you are a murderer, you had an abortion, you are addicted to pornography, you can't be faithful to one person, you are ugly, you were abused as a child, you have gone through a divorce…and if none of these types of condemning messages work then; HEY you don't even know what you are saying—you're just babbling," if we (as candidates) begin to speak in tongues! Some times we may even be too ashamed or timid to verbalize these deep-seated thoughts. Again, spirit-filled prayer warriors with the gift of the word of knowledge, can discern these tormenting, condemning spirits and their false and accusatory messages. I believe this is a good time to interject an important quote from one of my spiritual collaborators of this book, Min. Z. Maddox, *"We allow guilt and condemnation to hinder us from receiving the Holy Spirit because we judge ourselves by our performance; but God judges our HEART. God said we all have fallen short of His glory. He knows we will make mistakes; however, He will not hold our transgressions against us. He has forgave us for our past, present and future sins over 2000, years ago."*

Guided prayers leading us in confessions can purge minds of and free souls from those oppressive spirits (or ***hook up*** blockers) that are there to definitely condemn us and scramble the signal or jam the reception of the baptism.

Deliverance

Clean Vessels through Deliverance

Purging prayers can sometimes lead to something deeper called Deliverance. Deliverance is a way of cleaning out our earthly houses and inviting the Holy Spirit in. While God will accept us as we are, that is no excuse to STAY as we are. Deliverance is necessary for many of us because the enemy can use out not being delivered as a tool to either prevent us from receiving the Holy Ghost Hook up or to hinder us in our walk after we have received. Let's say that the President was coming to visit, we would want him to come to a clean house, right? Then why invite the Holy Spirit into a dirty one? Or let's say we were covered with mud from head-to-toe, would we then put on clean, expensive clothes without first cleaning up? My point is, if we have not been cleaned and purged of unclean spirits that oppress and negatively influence us then we are merely attempting to "dress a mess" because those spirits are still in there. The act of "Dressing a mess" is further demonstrated by a story I once heard.

There was a soldier at war who was hit by ammunition that fragmented in his leg. The doctor had an assistant who assumed all of the fragments had been removed and attempted to dress the wound. The skilled doctor, stopped the assistant, took a scalpel and a pair of tongs and began digging to locate the last piece of fragment in the wounded soldier's leg, which he expertly removed. Then he permitted his assistant to clean and dress the wound. Later he explained that if he had allowed the assistant to dress the wound without removing that fragment, the wound would have become infected and the soldier could have eventually become crippled or could have died from infection.

By this story, I am reiterating the necessity of having prayer warriors who are well versed in the art of deliverance. Those warriors can skillfully lead candidates who desire to be filled with the Holy Spirit and are oppressed or under demonic influences to cleansing through deliverance. This is done by confessing, purging and renouncing anything that is not like God in their lives. The Holy Spirit **Hook Up** is designed so that the infilling will help us present **clean** vessels and clean hearts to God at the appointed time. Anything less than total deliverance could result in an infection that could spread throughout the church eventually causing many to be spiritually crippled or to die spiritual deaths.

Here's another thing, total deliverance can come in degrees or it can also be continuous; depending on what our spirits are exposed to during our spiritual walk. There are times when demonic influences come from unholy alliances, through ungodly practices such as adultery, fornication or soul ties. Additionally, those influences could come through ungodly practices of psychic activities or hypnosis. They can even be established through near death experiences that introduce a spirit of fear or by laying hands on others who are operating under the influence of demonic or unclean spirits. And the list goes on.

These are also reasons that deliverance warriors or believers working with those under the influence of evil or unclean spirits, should not touch candidates until the Holy Spirit leads them to. Also there are areas where candidates should **NOT** be touched, as they are a point of spiritual expelling as well as transference. Rubbing the middle of candidates' backs, the nape of their necks or allowing candidates to hug prayer partners or warriors should be avoided at all times—if there is evidence of suspected demonic or spiritual manifestations.

Now this deliverance information is not being shared to sound ***weird*** or ***spooky*** but the Bible clearly illustrates proper deliverance methods in expelling unclean spirits from those that Jesus and Paul prayed for. There is a right way and a ***wrong*** way.

I recall the story of the 7 sons of Sceva who tried unsuccessfully to emulate Jesus and Paul's deliverance ministry but according to the Word, they were beaten so badly by evil spirits that they fled out of the house naked (Acts 19:16).

Ministering deliverance and engaging in spiritual warfare are a part of the prayer warriors' job that is the most undesirable and unsought. When spirits manifest and come out they can also be accompanied by some disturbing behaviors like vomiting, loud screeching, profanity, or secreting extreme amounts of mucus. I have seen these manifestations and others that I will not share at this time to avoid examples that could provoke fear or be too graphic.

Some prayer warriors through the gift of discernment can actually see the spirits hiding just beneath the surface of candidates' eyes. They can command the evil or unclean spirit to reveal their name through the word of wisdom. The authority of the Name of Jesus Christ should be used to expel the unclean spirits. Furthermore, the deliverance should only be ministered by those who are "prayed and fasted up" to prevent a Sceva-type experience.

As a young Christian, I remember telling my prayer warring partners that I didn't want to see, sense or even ***discern*** a spirit! Now, after working with hundreds to receive the Baptism of the Holy Spirit over the years, I can definitively say that being able to do so can often save much time in the ***Hook up*** process!

Fear or Faith

Sometimes interference can come from something as simple as a candidate's fear of the unknown. We have to understand that fear and faith cannot operate in the same realm. During these times, it is important for the prayer warrior to speak the Word of God that produces faith when fear tries to attack. The Bible also tells us that Perfect love casts out all fear. And where is perfect love found? We find it in God and His Holy Word.

Another interference is when self-intellect comes into play and the candidate tries to figure out what is being said when the Holy Spirit starts to speak through him or her. By praying, quoting Scriptures, laying hands on candidates and binding doubt and confusion, a prayer warrior can often help to alleviate these obstructions in the flow without time-consuming "tarrying-type" activities. We now know that the "old school" marathon tarrying in is not necessary. This was a practice that was erroneously carried over from the Book of Luke when the believers were instructed to tarry (wait) in Jerusalem. They were told to wait only until they were given the promised power from on High. The promise and the power were sent to us on The Day of Pentecost. Since that time we ***do not*** have to tarry or wait to be filled with the Holy Ghost. It is important to be confidently sure that the only things required of us are to believe and receive. The power has already been given to us. We just need to let the Holy

Spirit have His way within us ***TODAY.*** As a believer there is nothing else to wait for. Remember, the promise is for as "...***many as the Lord our God shall call".*** (Acts 2:39)

Prayer Warriors

The Prayer Warriors Don't Give the Holy Spirit

Another widespread inaccuracy in the church is that the prayer warriors or prayer partners ***give*** candidates the Holy Spirit. Prayer warriors just like any believer merely join their gift of faith with the candidates' and act as "Holy Ghost Cheerleaders" encouraging and spiritually watching for their souls. Even so, there are also many people who have received the baptism of the Holy Spirit without **anyone** else laying hands on them or being around. As some folks say, "God is God and He can do whatever He wants to do"—that includes how we receive the ***Holy Ghost Hook up***!

A short while ago a young lady asked me, "How long have you been giving people the baptism of the Holy Ghost?" I quickly responded, "I never have." I explained to her that I pray in agreement and in faith for people to receive the baptism of the Holy Ghost from God. That is it in a nutshell. Prayer warriors are there to pray, to lay hands, to loose strongholds and to inspire candidates to accept and receive the gift of the Holy Spirit that has already been given to them. But always keep in mind that people can also pray ALONE and receive the Baptism of the Holy Ghost if they are believers. Having a prayer warrior pray with you is not the only way and may not be THE BEST WAY for you. Even this could be a hindrance for some. There are those who are private, or self-conscious and might do better seeking the ***hook up*** on their own.

My husband and I were at a Montgomery for Jesus Rally listening to Donnie McClurkin singing when I heard the Holy Spirit tell me to look at my husband. When I turned to him, I saw him standing there next to me tearfully speaking in his Heavenly prayer language. No one ever laid hands on him. He was so engrossed in praising God during the praise and worship service that He was totally open to receive.

Again, remember there are many people who have received the baptism of the Holy Spirit while they were by themselves. God's sovereignty grants Him the right to do whatever He wants. We should never try to fit God or His Holy Ghost into a box because as the Creator God has also created "thinking outside the box." Many of us have heard it said that God "can save by many or save by few." I totally agree with that. As our ultimate Supplier and our Provider, God is in charge. That is why all the glory for our divine ***hook up*** to the Baptism of the Holy Spirit in our lives has to go to Him. No prayer warrior, minister or even Pastor can share in this glory. We can plant and we can water but God ultimately grants the increase.

The Prayer Warrior Can Help Lead Us There But We Are The Receivers

Without doubt, prayer warriors will and should pray in the Spirit when they work with candidates. However, they cannot MAKE anyone else speak in tongues. They can command the enemy to loosen tongues but again the ultimate action is between the Holy Ghost and the person who is seeking to be filled. ***We*** must open our **own** mouths and let the rivers of living water flow out from **our** bellies.

One member of my church to this very day claims that I choked the tongues out of him. When I prayed for him to receive, he was not speaking but the Holy Spirit let me know the words were in his throat waiting to come out. I put my hands on his neck (maybe a little firmly) commanding the devil to "loose his tongue". He began speaking in one of the most beautiful prayer languages I have heard. He just needed a little ... ah ... encouragement. I did not *make* that brother speak in tongues. We have to be willing to relinquish control of the most *unruly* member of our bodies—our tongues (James 3:8). The devil wont mind taking control yet God is a perfect gentleman and because He is, we have to be willing to let His Spirit in so that we can receive all that God has in store for us.

Today, if any of us inherited a billion dollars and it was deposited into a financial institution, we would first have to come forth in our authority proclaiming our identity to obtain the inheritance. Likewise, spiritually, we have to know who we are in God. Our Father has proclaimed that we are His children, His *"heirs and joint-heirs with Christ"*. (Romans 8:17) Consequently, we should have no problem with authoritatively confessing that we are Christian believers or that Jesus is Lord of our lives.

The next step we take in claiming our inheritance is essential. We must accept and receive the manifestation or the substance of it or else the inheritance will stay right where it is! Just imagine all the things that a billion dollars could have bought—benefits that could have been ours for the taking—that never would be apprehended if we refuse to hold our hands out and ***accept*** that rightful inheritance. Applying this principle spiritually, we can see how one of the most crucial elements in obtaining the **Holy Ghost Hook up** and Baptism of the Holy Spirit is being willing to receive it.

Just Do It!

As candidates for the baptism of the Holy Ghost: lift their arms in an upward position, outstretched to the Lord, I often tell them that this action is like that of a television antenna that helps the receiver to get better reception to accept the signal—and in this case from Heaven. Then I ask them to picture themselves receiving the Holy Ghost signal straight from God Almighty. I also ask them to try to imagine the love Jesus must have had when He stretched His arms and died on Calvary for all of our sins. I remind them that this was done so that we would be able to freely receive God's promise of the Baptism of the Holy Spirit. At that very moment all the candidate has to do is believe and receive. It is at this point that I encourage them to open their mouths by faith and audibly verbalize whatever the Holy Spirit is prompting them to say. If they are obedient, usually the next words that follow are not in English. In most cases, the next words are the Heavenly prayer language that they have been blessed to receive.

I'll end with this story of a 9-year-old whose Mom had just been blessed to receive the ***Holy Ghost Hook Up*** after years of going unsuccessfully to the altar and praying with others to receive. After we successfully prayed together, she went home to share her blessed experience with her family. It so impacted this little young man that he came to church the next night with his Mom literally demanding to be filled too. He didn't know much of anything except the wonderful change he witnessed in his mother and that he wanted to be changed as well. Failure was not an option. He came in child-like faith and received the Baptism within minutes. Let me tell you that there wasn't a dry eye in the church! I know that what God did for that little guy, He can do for anyone who believes.

It is my prayer that after reading this booklet, every believer knows with any doubt that they can receive the baptism of the Holy Spirit with the initial evidence of speaking in tongues immediately. I pray that they believe that they no longer have to tarry or wait.

After having been made aware of the hindrances, the misinformation, the need for deliverance and the purpose of prayer warriors, we should likewise understand that it is not necessary to wait until the next church service. It is not even necessary to even go to the church to receive the baptism of the Holy Spirit. God can bless you right here and right now. So why wait? The Bible tells us that Jesus is already there making intercession for each of us. (Romans: 8:34, ***It is Christ that died, yea rather, that is risen again, who is even at the right hand of God, who also maketh intercession for us***).

My final question is directed to those who are reading this booklet and have not yet been filled with the baptism of the Holy Ghost. A*re* ***you*** ***ready to receive your full inheritance***? If your answer is yes, just begin by telling God you are ready for the Holy Ghost **Hook Up** and then prepare to **RECEIVE.** If you are truly ready, go ahead and put your hands up in the air **RIGHT NOW**. This signifies surrender to the God Almighty. Next, honestly confess, *"**Holy Spirit, I am ready to receive a signal of communication directly from God and speak to Him in my Heavenly prayer language. Father God, I ask forgiveness and to be cleansed from all my sins by the blood of Jesus Christ of Nazareth. I claim and accept Jesus as my Lord and Savior and as a believer; I now receive the baptism of the Holy Spirit!**"*

Now, if you are seeking the Holy Ghost Hook up and are more comfortable obtaining assistance from a spirit-filled prayer warrior or a believer to help with the process, that is perfectly fine and acceptable. You may have tried unsuccessfully or you may feel that additional deliverance is needed. To you I say, let the Lord lead you. God will meet you wherever you are. He has given you a measure of faith so use it.

Whatever method you choose, I guarantee you that at the very moment you believe, you shall receive the Holy Ghost Hook up. After which, all that is left to do is to enjoy your direct communication and fellowship with God!

Hook Up Assessment

1. What is a hook up? An ________ term used to ________ helping ______ ______ ______ desired _______ or _______ for _______.

2. What is a Holy Ghost Hook up?

3. A. □ The Baptism of the HS B. □ A Prayer

4. Name just three inner issues that people may make people feel that they can't access God?

   a. ___________________________________

   b. ___________________________________

   c. ___________________________________

5. What are two reasons that people might say they have the Holy Spirit but have no prayer language?

   a. E_ _ _ _ ***and*** b. E_ _ _ _ _ _

6. When we receive the baptism of the Holy Ghost, we ALWAYS receive the prayer language.

   □ True or □ False

7. Name five reasons why we should not just pray in English? ______________________________

   ____

   ____

8. Give three trains of thought that can contributed to strongholds and condemnation

   U_ _ _ _ _ _ U_ _ _ _ _ _ _ _ &

   U _ _ _ _ _ _ _ _ _ _ _

9. According to ***Acts 2:38b-39a*** who is the promise for? ______________________________

   ____

   ____

10. Write down some "programmed" messages that Satan could try to use against you to "jam" your receiving the baptism of the Holy Ghost?

____

____

____

11. What is Deliverance?

____

____

12. In your own words, what does it mean to "dress a mess?

____

____

____

13. What two things cannot operate in the same realm?

    a. Fear and Fasting

    b. Faith and Fellowship

    c. Faith and Fear

14. We must tarry for the Baptism of the Holy Ghost.

    □ True or □ False

15. Can someone receive the baptism of the Holy Spirit without anyone praying for them or laying hands on them?

    □ Yes or □ No

16. When you receive the Baptism all glory goes to whom? ____________________

17. What is the most unruly member of our bodies according to James 3:8? Our ________________

18. Name something a prayer warrior does do.

    ____

19. Name something a prayer warrior does NOT do.

____

20. What posture of prayer denotes surrender?

____

Important Spiritual Dates

Salvation: ______________________________

Water Baptism: ___________________________

Baptism of the Holy Spirit: __________________

The Key to a successful Spiritual Walk is...

BALANCE

God first

Family Second

Ministry Third

Additional Ways to Maintain The Holy Ghost Hookup

- Read the Word of God Every Day
- Pray Daily in the Holy Spirit
- Regularly Fast
- Join a Church (as the Holy Spirit Leads)
- Volunteer to Serve in a Church Ministry
- Fellowship with Other Believers
- Repent for Sins of Omission and Commission Daily
- Lead Someone Else to Christ
- Support The Church Financially through Tithes and Offerings

Counting Blessings

First

For God: He gave creation and salvation.

Second

For children: they gave purpose.

Third

For soul mates: they gave love.

Fourth

For Moms and Dads: they gave life.

Fifth

For life: it gave experience.

Sixth

For wisdom: it gave direction.

Seventh

For God's Word: it gave faith.

Eight

For the Holy Spirit: He gave instruction.

Bibliography

Scriptures quoted from the King James Version of the Holy Bible - The Holy Bible, New King James Version® Copyright © 1982 by Thomas Nelson, Inc.; The New American Standard Bible Copyright © 1995; and other versions - All rights reserved.

Every effort was made to properly attribute the sources of all quoted materials to this book. The quotes are in most cases, exact quotations, however, some have been edited for clarity and brevity—but in all cases, an attempt has been made to maintain the speaker's original intent. In some cases quoted material for the book was obtained from secondary sources, including print media and online websites'. Although every effort was made to ensure the accuracy of the sources and attribution of the quotes, it cannot be guaranteed. I believe all materials (Bible reference and quotations) contained herein are accurate, and I shall not be held liable for the same. If I have overlooked anything, please contact me. I will every attempt to make any corrections deemed necessary in future editions.

Cathy Nored (CN Nomoor)

Other Books Available On www.lulu.com:

Also Available...

www.ingramcontent.com/pod-product-compliance
Ingram Content Group UK Ltd.
Pitfield, Milton Keynes, MK11 3LW, UK
UKHW020217250726
13967UKWH00001B/57
9 781300 158769